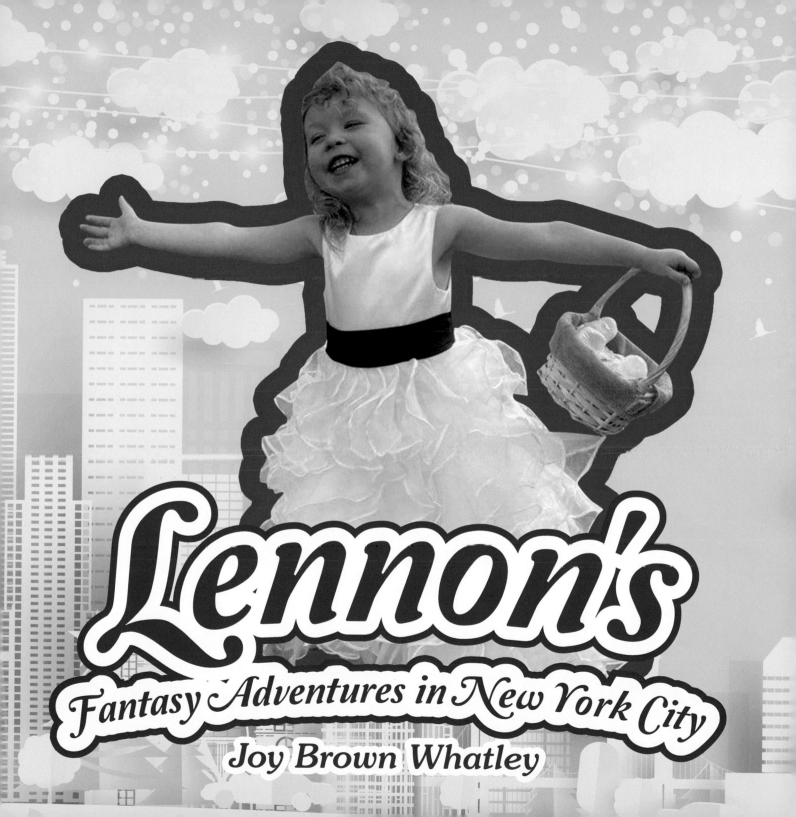

Lennon's
Fantasy Adventures in New York City
Joy Brown Whatley

To order additional copies of this book, contact:
Xlibris
844-714-8691
www.Xlibris.com
Orders@Xlibris.com

ISBN: Softcover   978-1-6698-0375-1
        Hardcover   978-1-6698-0376-8
        EBook   978-1-6698-0374-4

Print information available on the last page

Rev. date: 02/22/2022

Monday

In New York City

*L*ennon woke up this MONDAY MORNING seeing the rain coming down outside her bedroom window. "I know what I will do, I will take a pretend trip for an adventure in my mind."

First, she grabbed her beautiful backpack and started packing all her make-up. She loved all the pretty items and then she carefully measured them for the flight to NEW YORK CITY.

She wondered why did they call it the big apple. On the map it didn't look like an apple. She took time to check with Google about that question. She found out that a reporter had written an article, way back in 1924, about the dream of every horseman racing was to go to the Big Apple. She was pleased to find that Google had so much information.

Now, on with her packing. All of these beautiful clothes to pack. How would she ever decide which ones to take on this exciting trip.

Her next decision was whether she wanted to fly on the back of a big bird like her cousin, Jaxon did in his fantasy adventures or did she want to fly by plane. Since she had never been on an airplane, she decided that is what she would do.

Lennon made all the arrangements and booked her flight to New York City. Of course, she would have a stop in Atlanta, but that was okay.

It was getting time for her taxi and she was packed and ready to go. It was a very nice trip and she enjoyed watching all the beautiful fluffy clouds as she traveled across the sky. As they started to land, all of the buildings seem to reach way up into the sky. Lennon was so excited.

Lennon went straight from her taxi to her hotel room in Times Square. What a busy, beautiful place, with so much activity all around her. Where did she want to eat? McDonald's or a fancy place? She decided to get a hamburger and rest up for her adventures for tomorrow.

She looked out the window about midnight and people were walking around all over the place. What were all these people doing in the middle of the night? This was a very active place, day or night.

Tuesday

In New York City

Tuesday morning came with all the excitement of all the adventures Lennon would have today.

Lennon decided on one of the tourist buses. She went to the top deck to travel to the Empire State Building. It was so tall, that people looked like ants on the sidewalk below. She enjoyed looking out over the big city from this tall building.

She found walking around in this big city was so much fun, with so many things to see. She walked past the Trump Hotel. Wow, what a grand place to stay. She wondered why she had not booked that hotel. Oh well, the price of $616 per night sounded like a lot of money. She was happy to be staying in Times Square.

Although Lennon didn't need any new clothes, she was having so much fun shopping in these fancy stores, she ended up buying more stuff. A lot of make-up and clothes to carry back home to Alabama.

Wednesday

In New York City

TODAY, Lennon would travel on a bus to Ellis Island to visit the Statue of Liberty. She found out that the Statue of Liberty was 305-foot-high, including the base. It had been given to the United States by France as a symbol of the two countries friendship. It was created way before Lennon was born, back in 1875. She also, learned that the Statue of Liberty has been recognized across the world as a beacon of freedom, welcoming people around the world to New York City.

Some women didn't like the statue of a woman being used, when back in those days, women didn't even have the right to vote. Lennon was so glad that had changed. Lennon thought, I might run in the election for President of the United State in 2075. Lennon thought that there are so many vocations a woman can have now. She thought I might even be a doctor, like my great, great, great grandfather, Dr. Bryan Boroughs was back when there were only a few physicians in Alabama. Life is so exciting, thinking about all the great choice she can have in this modern day that we live.

Thursday

In New York City

Lennon was up bright and early, ready for another adventure. She went to Central Park, where she encountered many interesting sights. She saw some dogs and dog owners pulling on their animals. The dogs always seemed to want to go the opposite direction.

She went to the Central Park Zoo first, since she loved animals and enjoyed watching them. Lennon spent hours watching all the different animals, but her favorite was the sea lion, playing in the Sea Lion Pool.

While at Central Park she decided to try ice skating for the first time in her life. She found that the skates slid across the ice and down she went. She fell down several times before she finally zoomed around like an expert. That was an exciting adventure.

The lake was beautiful and eating at the Lakeside Restaurant was a real treat.

No visit to Central Park would be complete without riding on the Carousel. Oh, what fun she had. This was a great day in New York City.

Friday

In New York City

FRIDAY, was Lennon's big day to go to a Broadway Show. Mary Poppins was the musical she decided to attend. She was amazed how the nanny could fly around with her umbrella and not fall. She was not sure how that the law of gravity didn't seem to work here. They were able to show things happening that seemed impossible. Lennon was good at pretending but all of this seemed to be real. The pretty nanny for these wealthy children seemed to be so much fun, thinking of all the hilarious things to do. Lennon was impressed and fell in love with the show.

What a great Friday in New York City.

Saturday

In New York City

Today was Saturday and Lennon was thinking about all the places she had seen and all the fun things she had done this week. Lennon thought I would like to do some normal things today, like sitting in the sand and digging with a little shovel at the beach. To her surprise she didn't have to go very far to find a kid's park with some water and sand. Dressed in her cutest swimsuit, she sat down and started digging, putting the sand in her little pail. To her amazement, she started digging up beautiful diamonds, rubies and pearls. Wow! What a surprise, all these beautiful shiny, jewels. She gathered up the jewels by the handful and placed them in her pail. Now, "I am rich," she yelled. It was so exciting to find all these jewels in the sand.

What an exciting week Lennon had enjoyed.

Sunday

In New York City

This week of fantasy adventures was about to come to an end. Every day had been different and so much fun. Now it was Sunday. Lennon didn't know where she wanted to go to church, but she thought she would go to one close to Times Square. She felt at home in this huge church. Since she knew all the songs she could enjoy singing with this beautiful music. The people were nice and friendly, which surprised her in this big city.

After church, she went to The Capital Grille, for lunch. It was good and very expensive. Lennon didn't care about money. She was rich with all her jewels she had found. She could buy anything she wanted.

Lennon spent part of her Sunday enjoying a nice rest. After her nap, it was time to get a taxi and leave for the airport. She would be in Atlanta soon and one hour later be back in Mobile.

Lennon had enjoyed doing so many amazing things. This was a wonderful pretend trip. Now, it had stopped raining and it was time to see what she could do in the real world. Lennon was happy to enjoy the many pleasures life has provided, in real life and in her fantasy world.

Printed in the United States
by Baker & Taylor Publisher Services